Psalms

For The 21st Century

By

The Reverend Leslie L. Booker

PSALMS FOR THE 21ST CENTURY

Copyright © 2011

The Reverend Leslie L. Booker

ISBN: 978-0-9816838-1-2

Published by
Sherrill Enterprises
PO Box 3372
Mount Vernon, NY 10553

Cover Design: Elsa Forsythe & Peter Sherrill

Back cover photo by Shellian Rodney

DEDICATION

Psalms for the 21st Century is dedicated to my maternal grandmother, Clara White, affectionately known as Bammy, who loved and nurtured me, encouraged me, supported me, and taught me to love God, to pursue my dreams and to never give up until I found what I was looking for. She is the person who fostered in me a love for the written word, teaching me to read at age four and taking me through the kindergarten curriculum before I entered the public school system. She was an avid reader who was always seeking knowledge that would make life better for herself and those she encountered. I had the privilege of her unconditional love and support as well as the wisdom of a life well lived until she went home to be with her first love, Jesus Christ, in September 1995 at the young age of 104. Although her physical presence is missed greatly, she has left an eternal heritage that will live on. This book is a testimony of her legacy.

BIOGRAPHY

Reverend Leslie Booker (who also writes under the pen name *Tulani*) is an ordained Christian minister and poet who currently serves on the ministerial staff of New Life Fellowship in Mount Vernon, New York as the New Members Class instructor and Adult Sunday School teacher. Her spiritual journey began in childhood with the guidance of her maternal grandmother, Clara White, who constantly modeled a Christian life of service and continuously taught her to love God and to serve Him. The unconditional love she received from her grandmother and the witness of this love toward others was a powerful testimony and motivated her to seek to know God on a more intimate level. Eventually, this quest led to answering the call to ministry and she was ordained in November 2001 at Nothing Impossible Fellowship, Reston, Virginia.

Her poetry is another aspect of her ministry that has emerged as an avenue to inspire and bless others. Reverend Booker recalls, "In 1983 during a time of prayer and worship, I was directed to read Psalm 26:7,"… that reads as follows, "That I may publish with the voice of thanksgiving and tell of all thy wondrous works." (KJV). It was many years later that I discovered that poetry was the medium. I write under the pen name Tulani which means one who brings peace. Since childhood, I have had a lifelong interest and love of literature, poetry, rhythm and words. I have always been fascinated by words, their many shades of meaning, and the inherent rhythm that the spoken word conveys. I write about life experiences—mine and others. This includes our spiritual relationship with our Creator. Anything that gets my attention can be a source of inspiration. I use words to create pictures in the minds of readers and hearers that they can relate to with the hope that they will be encouraged to believe for a better future."

Reverend Leslie Booker is a gifted bible teacher and retreat and workshop leader who was born in Manhattan and educated in the New York City public schools. She has lived in California, Kentucky, Ohio and Virginia. She has been active in community development and ministry for many years and has served in many capacities. These include founding The Shepherd's Staff Ministry, Inc., Mount Vernon, New York; a ministry of restoration to those needing emotional healing, founding member of Christ Fellowship Church, Herndon, Virginia, Regional Prayer Coordinator for the 1986 Billy Graham Crusade, Washington, D.C., Community

Development Specialist, Early Childhood Teacher, Board Member Fairfax Community Action Program and Falls Church Head Start Program (Fairfax, Virginia).

Additionally, she has worked as executive support for the Academic Vice President, SUNY Old Westbury, New York, the Canon Missioner of the Washington National Cathedral and the Vice President of Prison Fellowship International. Reverend Booker recently retired from the General Board of Global Ministries of The United Methodist Church where she also served on the Staff Association Executive Board and the Negotiations Committee.

ABOUT THE BOOK

"Poetry is making music with words."

Poetry is a gift that touches the hearts of people in a similar way that music does. It crosses all boundaries of life and circumstances. Psalms for the 21st Century was written during a very intense time of emotional loss. My journey from despair to joy is expressed through poetry. My struggle to heal and the journey I had to take to find wholeness is depicted throughout every poem. The joy of finally being set free is evident and transcends the struggle. Every reader will be able to identify with some part of my journey and hopefully be encouraged to press on to final victory.

This book of poetry is written to encourage all those who have struggled with the perplexities and vagaries of life and been wounded by encounters with others. Many experiences in my personal life forced me to find a way to express the potent emotions and pain that are stirred when life situations present themselves with no visible answers. I cried out to the God who created me to come and turn my desert places into well watered gardens. My prayer is that everyone who reads this book will see that they are not alone in their struggles because there is a God who loves and cares for them and who will sustain them on their journey to wholeness. He is our only hope and we must return again and again to the One who is love to fill us with the life-giving water that quenches our thirst.

ACKNOWLEDGEMENTS

I want to thank God who through His son Jesus Christ who has given me eternal life and the gift of poetry to share with the world.

Many thanks to my dear friend and fellow author, Randolph Whitney Cameron, who faithfully helped me find the courage to actually use my gift to write poetry and to believe that one day I would see it in print.

I want to give special accolades to my publisher, Peter Sherrill of Sherrill Enterprises, for being my constant and faithful coach in helping me to give birth to Psalms for the 21st Century. Thank you for all your support and gentle prodding to get to work whenever I became complacent. You are truly an extraordinary person who gets things done in a timely and orderly way. Thank you for being such an integral part of the process. Without you, the book would still be in gestation.

To my family and friends who have loved and supported me throughout this process as I attempted to fulfill my destiny, may you reap the fruit of your labor and fulfill your dreams. Thank you from the bottom of my heart and may God bless you.

TABLE OF CONTENTS

Prologue: A paradox—crook and cross. At first glance, they seem to be contradictory. They become one as the cross becomes the instrument of transformation of the other (crook).

THE CROOK AND THE CROSS

Jesus, the shepherd, looks longingly at his flock.
Roll call begins.
Are all here? Are any missing?
A wee one's faint cry is heard in the distance.
Drowned out by the noise of the other sheep
As they shove—baa and bleat.
Only the shepherd's ear is turned toward the cry.
Wolves lurk outside the sheep pen
Circling the little one—teeth bared.
Snarls and grunts crescendo as they close
In on their prey.
Hopelessness and despair abound.
No hope for the wee one to be found.
The sound of a trumpet is heard!
All ears become alert.
Still the little one is bound.
Fear closes out all sound
But the beating of a frenzied heart.
Body frozen as if sculptor hewn.
Who can set the captive free?
Will it be Jesus working through me?
Hark! I hear my master's call.
Take my crook and rescue all.
I died to set the captives free.
Pick up your cross and follow me.

Epilogue: In grateful thanksgiving from one crook (who has broken God's law) to another whose crook rescues the lost. The shepherd's crook is used as an extension of one's self. May we all become extensions of Christ as we pick up our cross (an instrument of transformation) daily and follow him.

Prologue: "You will be like a well watered garden, like a spring whose waters never fail." (Isiah. 58:11c - NIV)

MORNING OF LIFE

Awakened at the crack of dawn
Excitement in my heart.
Night air shifting to the freshness
Of a new day.
Expectation rising
To consciousness.
Breathing deeply
Pure air filling my lungs.
Sky a kaleidoscope of shapes and color;
Changing rapidly
Like scenes in a play.
Birds flitting here and there.
Now you see them
Then they're gone.
Night owls resting.
Sweet songs of praise
Rising upward.
Sea breezes cresting air's currents
Reminiscent of days past
Reminder of future joys
Still to come.
Strength for the future
Crescendos forth from
Fire's ashes left from long ago.
Hope,
Joy,
Zest for living,
Overflows my being
Waters the deserts
Of the thirsty.

Epilogue: I will say of the Lord, He is my fortress and my rock.
(Psalms. 31:3 - NIV)

Prologue: Jesus said to them, "My food is to do the will of Him who sent me, and to accomplish His work." (John 4:34 - NAS)

TO BE CONTINUED

Like chapters in a book
Life continues to grow.
Nobody told me so
I just know—
Plumbs the depths of
Worlds shared.
Pain bared
By many.
Excited by vast reaches
Of vistas unknown.
Universe creating
Making pictures
Still unseen,
Unfolds daily
Moment by moment.
Happening like heartbeats
One-two, one-two, one-two.
Steady and sure.
Pure in its purpose.
Foreign bodies left to macrophages
Whose job it is to
Devour the intruders.
Stirred by rhythms written
On the essence of being,
Currents of love move us gently forward.

Epilogue: Written to all those experiencing transition.

Prologue: This is written to those still seeking their identity and to those who have found themselves. May they continue in hope as life continues to cause their metamorphosis.

WHAT'S IN A NAME?

What difference does a name make?
Conceived in darkness,
Bathed in light,
Cast from blindness
into sight.
Welcomed by some,
Rejected by many.
Is it any wonder
So many cut asunder?
Hitchhiking through life's circumstances.
Labels changing like price tags in the local supermarket.
Answering to others perceptions
Hurling at us
From many directions.
How to find ourselves?
That's the real question.
Looking here and there
Following paths
Left unclear
By the guide
Who's gone on to better things
While we flounder
Caught within
The thickets of life's
Brambles,
Like yarn the cat got hold of.
How to find ourselves?
That's the real question.
Look within not without.
Be still – don't shout!
Listen, listen, listen
To the heart's song.
Can you hear the drumbeat
Making unique sounds
All your own,

4

WHAT'S IN A NAME (CONT'D.)

Feet tapping rhythms
In harmony with your soul?
Music designed
To put the pieces back
And make you whole.
Spirit, soul, and body
One in thanksgiving,
Sing, "Holy, Holy, Holy
Unto the Lord."

Epilogue: A rose, is a rose, is a rose by any name. The essence within
defines its being not the name others give to it.

Prologue: A metamorphosis of life.

CHANGE

Change begins the moment
Of birth into the earth.
Spewed out of a safe haven
With force greater than
A tractor trailer
Whose brakes fail
While hurtling down a
Mountain side.
Out of control
Ours that is.
Landing in an environment
Not of our choosing.
Confusing – isn't it?
Nevertheless,
We grow.
One minute – speechless,
The next – words tumble
Out of our mouths
Faster than we can count them.
Some things stay the same.
Others remain unrecognizable
Bearing faint
Resemblance to the
Original creation.
The puzzle inside
Takes shape and form.
Integration is more than
Black and white
Mixed together.
Harmonious blending
Of a multicolor
Universe
Each color distinct
And complimentary to
All others

CHANGE (CONT'D.)

Seems like what the Creator had in mind.
So what if I like purple
And red's your favorite view?
Others being partial
To colors of another hue.
Does it really make
A difference
To the quality of life
We all talk about?
There comes a day
For each of us
When strife becomes
A footnote.
We're forced to look
Into the face of grace–
Personified.
Ready or not
Here we come
Out of control
Again.
The landscape of
Our lives
On display for all to see
No time now to
Touch up the picture.
What you see
Is what you get.
Death by any other name
Remains the same for all
A change unchangeable.
Warning!
To those whose picture is still
In process,
Paint yours
With living colors.
You'll live forever there.
Hope you like the view.

Epilogue: "…It is appointed unto man once to die, but after this the judgment." (Hebrews 9:27 – KIV)

Prologue: A heat wave, war in Bosnia and in other parts of the world, and a TV special about a WWII disaster on an island in the Pacific where over 20,000 U.S. Marines and soldiers died because of human pride – all attributed to the imagery of this poem.

HEAT WAVE

Shimmering waves of oppression
Undulating through the air
Crushing life's
Breath
Exposing bones bare.
Blurring our vision,
Searing our reason,
Obscuring the beauty
Of the landscape of lives thrown into chaos
By other's logic.
Ideological symbols clashing
Filling the atmosphere
With thrashings
Forcing us to cover our ears,
Hide our tears,
Bury our fears.
Drowning out the stillness
Of harmony within.
Leaving memories
Of desolate terrain.
Out of the ashes
A hint of spring
Stirs hope eternal.
We live.

Epilogue: Let Christ reign in our hearts.

Prologue: When hope is just a distant shadow.

FREEDOM

A caged bird sits
Waiting to be free
But silently crying,
"Who will rescue me?"
A hand reaches out
Opens up the door.
The caged bird sits wondering
"Isn't there more?"
Another sees the plight
Fright has blinded sight.
Shouts in loud acclaim,
"Things are not the same!"
The bird responds in glee,
"Will you rescue me?"

Along comes a child
Whose eyes are open wide
Wonders why the bird
Is sitting still inside.
"The door is open wide,
Why don't you come outside?
There's much you need to see
Come and follow me"

The bird replies,
"I hear your voice.
I feel your heart
Yet years of bondage
Have made it dark.
I long to see.
I yearn to follow.
Try as I might
I can only wallow.
My wings are clipped.
I cannot fly.
I'd love to join you
And soar the sky.

FREEDOM (CONT'D.)

Alas, I fear
I'm doomed to stay
Inside this cage
And waste away"

The little one steps in
Reaches out his hand
Lifts the bird close to his heart
Then steps outside again.

"You need not fear the light
Receive the gift of sight.
Your freedoms won
By Christ – God's son.
I'll hold you high
Until you fly."

Epilogue: "…those that hope in the Lord shall renew their strength. They will soar on wings like eagles; they will run and not grow weary, they will walk and not faint". (Is: 40:31 – NIV)

Prologue: "…It is appointed unto man once to die, but after this the
judgment." (Hebrews 9:27– KIV)

ALL RISE

In God we trust or so the motto goes.
Do we really believe it or
Is it just a pose?
When doubts arise,
In what direction do we see?
Do we look up to Heaven
And surrender without a plea?
Or do we look the other way
And continue with our say?
"I'm right, you're wrong!"
Judgment is our song
Put the blame on others,
Talk about our druthers.
A word of advice,
Everyone can use it.
Cast your lot with the Master.
He'll deliver you faster.
On the other hand,
The law of all the land
Will wrap you in bars of steel.
Really not such a good deal.
Jesus sets the captives free
All of us that's you and me.
He already paid the price.
Why not take His advice?
Lay your burdens
At his feet
His sweet relief
Can't be beat.
He'll take you in His loving arms
Calm your fears, stop all alarms,
Strengthen your heart,
And light the dark,
Set you on your feet anew
Refreshed as the morning dew.
Ready to journey again
With Him.

Prologue: "Come to me, all you who are weary and burdened, and I will give you rest." (Matthew: 11:28 – NIV)

This was written in memory of my grandmother "Bammy," whose light still shines in the darkness of this world and encourages us to come home.

THE GATHERING

They came from near and far
To gather round the star,
A light so bright and full of love
It drew them to their Creator above.
A beacon in the dark
That comforted many a heart.
An incandescent glow
That lighted the path below.
A kind word here,
A touch there.
Heart and hands
What a pair.
It can't be beat
For lighting a street
Fraught with shadows
Of darkness
And threatening clouds
Hovering around
Like a neon sound
Shouting rest for the weary.
Her light drew them on.
Fueled by love so great,
It overflowed the crate.
Living waters healing all that passed by.
Now the light is shining brighter.
No longer contained in earthen vessel.
Challenges us to wrestle with our fears,
Overcome our years
Of judgment,
Release the pain
And gain life eternal.

Epilogue: Jesus is the light of the world. (John 9:5)

IN CHARGE

Prologue: A reminder to each of us.

One day I put myself in charge of all life's little bouts.
I thought I could control my life and other's too, no doubt!
It's easier if I direct, I know the script so well.
Little did I know, I'd soon confront the hosts of hell.
At first it seemed to work just fine—being in charge all of the time.
The pieces fell in pleasant places
And I enjoyed all life's graces.

The view was great. I began to elate; my heart swelled with pride.
I was the boss! I was in charge! I invited others to ride.
I took the boat out to sea—all the others went with me.
The air was fresh, the water clear.
Everyone was standing near.
All was calm, no cause for alarm.
Without a warning, the sea began to swell.
I quickly thought," It'll stop, and all will be well."

What a mistake I was about to make.
The more I steered the harder it got to keep the boat in check.
To my dismay it began to sway and toss us all about.
The boat veered, others jeered, and I lost control.
Before a plan could form in my head, the sea became my bed.
I struggled just to stay afloat and keep my eyes on the boat.

All was lost, I thought!
Only the birds were near to hear.
I was all alone in the dark of night, that was very clear.
"Why, oh why, I began to cry, didn't you let me know
That if I forgot to consult with you everything else would go?"
I'd find myself all alone in the midst of a scary space.
And peace would flee amidst shouts of glee, as I strained to keep my pace.
It was long ago before the world was formed
That the Creator ordained the place
He had for me to fill on earth as an instrument of his grace.
It's only when I am grounded in him that I know I'll complete the race.
So open your ears, dry your tears, and look to the hills above
Where the rock of creation is waiting for you to express his infinite love.

TWISTED

Have you ever watched a
Snake slither?
Words aimed straight as an arrow
Hit their mark
Catapult the victim into an abyss.
Makes you wonder where
You put your survival gear.
Wilderness training has its merits.
Just when the guide appears
Pointing the way to the vanished path,
Barbed vessels send
You off the edge again
Floundering like a fish
Out of water
Eyes popping,
Arms flailing.
Reminds you of the time
You rode the merry-go-round
After dining on a heavy meal.

THE MAKING OF A STAR

A Tribute to a Friend

A star is shinning in the darkness.
Lighting our way as we travel earth's paths.
Drawing our eyes heavenward.
Beckoning us forward.
Reminding us of joy-filled laughter.
Times when spirits touched.
Hearts filled with our Creator's love.
Now when night falls and daylight's faded,
Temptation roams sowing seeds of fear.
We have only to look above and be reminded
Of the lives of many witnesses still near.
Each point of light reflects the Master.
Together brighten our day.
Jewels of hope fulfilled.
Cheering us on our way.
Eternally in our hearts.
Only a thought away.
God with us always.
Walks with us today.
Walks with us today.

IN TIME

Lateness not greatness
Makes a difference after all.
Only the answer,
When you rear the Master's call.
Open your ears,
Hear the sounds anew.
Open your eyes,
See the panoramic view.
Open your heart,
Receive a fresh start.
Embrace a love so great.
That waits, and waits, and waits.
Accept the offer,
Fill your coffer.
Angels, shout with glee
As you cry out,
"Receive me
Into your kingdom great."
Thank God, I'm not too late.

Epilogue: "Come to me, all you who are weary and are carrying heavy
burdens, and I will give you rest." (Matthew: 11:28 – NRSV)

ON TIME

Jesus, the shepherd, stands at the gate,
Calling out, "Come in, come in!
Before it's too late."
Crowds pushing, shoving, crying out,
"Wait for me, I've just begun to see.
Your light illuminates me."
Others at the back try another tack.
See no way of getting through,
The crowd has closed the gap.
Fall upon their faces,
Cast their hope on God's graces.
Angels part the way,
Clear a space so they
Can see the Master.
Lift them up above the crowd,
All heads now bowed in awe
Outcasts carried above the law.
Enter my kingdom, says He,
Prepared for all whose
Hearts will see!

Epilogue: Friends brought their paralytic friend to see Jesus. They   couldn't
get in so they made a hole in the roof and lowered him inside where
Jesus said, "I tell you, get up, take your mat and go home."
(Mark 2:11 – NIV)

NO TIME

Tossing, turning, yearning,
Twisting, listing, burning,
Floundering in the sea of death.
Oil slick aflame atop the water
Keeps us from the cool, pool below.
Cries of pain shooting over rocks
Like a waterfall plunging
Down the mountainside;
Wearing out the hard veneer.
Splash! Splash! Splash!
Grooves appear.
Like a chick pecking its outer shell,
The heart struggles to escape from Hell,
Race for time nears the finish line.
Stopwatch ticking—seconds left.
Will you make it?
You can't fake it!
Love is real.
Yield!
The play is over.
The curtains drawn.
Soon the stage is dark.
Too late to make your mark.
Molten sea burning.
Heart still yearning.
Tossing, twisting, turning.

Epilogue: "…inasmuch as it is appointed for men to die once and after
this comes judgment…" (Hebrew 9:27 – NAS)

18

Prologue: Letting go sure ain't easy!

HEALING

Journey on an unknown path
Many twists and turns.
Still the heart yearns
For a place of rest.
Promises made,
Promises broken.
Things of the heart
Still unspoken.
Cause us to stop along the way.
A voice within gently stirs us
To journey on another day.
Again and again we hear it say,
"Come unto me and rest.
Put me to the test.
Lay your burdens down
And journey on."

Epilogue: "There remains then a Sabbath rest for the people of God, for
anyone who enters God's rest also rests from his own works,
just as God did from His." (Hebrews 4:9-10 - NIV)

HEARTS CRY

"Rainbow, rainbow in the sky,
Why must my dreams float by
Like ethereal clouds' drifting sigh?"
Running, I leap to catch them.

"Water, water in the brook,
Why must I continue to look
For heartfelt hopes in life's own book?"
Yearning, I reach out and grasp them.

"Father, Father lofty and high
Who bottles every tear
And hears every cry."
Answering, your arms enfold me.

"Love, love, where can you be?
In the height of the mountains
Or the depth of the sea?"
Looking, you find me.

Epilogue: Written for those who are waiting for their ship to come in.

MISSED CONNECTIONS

Today I waited patiently to hear your voice,
Knowing, expecting, anticipating
Another time of sharing.
Never dreaming we'd miss each other again.
Fervently straining to reach this simple goal,
Looking for that special connection
Not a pot of coal.
I was there by the phone.
You were where you belonged.
Each was in their place.
Then fate interrupted
What was to be an act of grace.
Divisionary tactics began to happen then
They finally succeeded and
Now I'm asking, "When?"
What God purposed is always for the best.
It still will happen and this was just a test.
Patience is a virtue.
I know this to be true.
But it's very hard to come by
When I want to talk with you.
I accept this lesson today
Of my own accord.
I cannot open the way.
I console myself with good intention.
I trust you'll do the same.
The other forces attempted contention.
We are not to blame.
We'll talk again another day.
We'll each have our say.
The best things come to those who wait.
I'll see you soon and we'll partake
Of friendship's special ties.

Epilogue: We learn patience through afflictions.

BRIDE SONG

You are the harmony to my melody,
The bass to my treble,
The cover to my book,
The words of my testimony,
The raiment of my being.
Your love has filled me up.
My cup runs over with joy.
I rejoice in your presence
Forever.

LOST BUT NOT FORGOTTEN

A book once lost now found
Like kindred spirits bound.
A love affair no less
Than a long forgotten kiss.
Like an old friend's embrace
After a long forgotten chase,
We greet and meet
With love's sweet taste.

THE WELL

Finding it?
It ain't easy!
Looking in all the wrong places.
This way,
That way,
Anyway.
No wonder we've lost it.
Our direction, I mean.
Started out so easy
Or so it seemed.
Focused on one tree—ME.
Missed the forest
There for all to see.
Myriads of encounters with God—our creativity.
A tree alone cannot stand
But joined with others
Throughout the lands
Draws water from deep within.
Enough to quench our thirst
And start again.
There's strength in numbers
And power to resist
The urge to halt our seeking
And sink into the eternal abyss.
Draw strength from one another.
Lean close and close the gap.
Leave no room for outside forces
To deposit their negative rap.
Lift voices high in praises.
Leave truth with all you meet.
Bow down before the Savior
And worship at His feet.
It's there we taste of heaven.
Our vision becomes clear.
We see the place we occupy
On this terra firma sphere.
We draw the living water
That only Christ can bring.

THE WELL (CONT'D.)

Returning to the forest
Renewed with strength within.
We take our place among the weak,
Those dying from their thirst.
Our frontier bursts and overflows
To those who need it most.
So all are quenched
And none left dry.
When we seek the fountain daily,
Then none will thirst and die!

Prologue: This is written about my beautiful granddaughters, Kayla
Camille Sizemore and Cassidy Lynn Sizemore.

A DOUBLE PORTION

I have lived to see a portion
Of eternity extended.
A part of me projected into time
Again and then again.
Little atoms forming
Then joining into shapes unknown.
Seeds planted long ago bearing fruit
At once familiar but different.
Now and then I see a glimpse
Of what was and is to come.
A new hope in a future yet unseen
Brings me joy unspeakable that overflows
Into punctuated praise and thanksgiving.
Producing a unique song that sails upward to the throne.
Where grace and mercy sit entwined
Within loves' holy presence.
I bow down and worship.
Amen! Amen! Amen!

METAMORPHOSIS II

Like a butterfly whose wings were clipped,
I was falling.
Drifting like a leaf on the soft autumn breeze.
One minute floating,
The next plunging to destruction.
See-Saw, Majorie Daw.
Motion sickness slowly rising to cloud my vision.
Stop, I cried, and let me off this heaving mountain.
Earth that refuses to be still.
Best intentions quickly tumbling.
Fractured pieces scattered wildly.
Can Humpty Dumpty be put together again?
Who can make the picture whole?
Resurrect my damaged soul?
Messiah, Messiah, quickly come.
Save me, Christ, whose victory is won.

FAMILY

Fractured pieces from a broken mold
Once royal vessels—then sold.
Unwilling travelers scattered abroad
Struggle to survive—while buried alive.
No mother's arms to comfort them.
Only waves crashing and a terrifying end.
Words thrown out disappear in the air
Have nowhere to land no ear to hear.
Agonizing cries burst from within
Where darkness and grief form a cauldron of heat.
Molecules and atoms dancing a score of despair.
The tempo increases.
The pot overflows.
Chaos ensues and then the death blows.
Some to the ocean and others to land.
Bodies and souls perish and others still stand.
Shells now empty with no sense of self.
Exploited by aliens who rake in the wealth.
From this spawns a nation sowing seeds inhumane.
Corruption and killing lead to mayhem.
Mother Earth is writhing prepared to give birth.
What shall we expect but more funeral dirge?
Something must change but where do we start?
First things first it must start in our heart.

CHOICES

Words gentle as a cool summer's breeze
Hold us, caress us, put us at ease.
Others hurl through the air like arrows flung into space,
Surely not an instrument of grace.
Pierce us, wound us, cause us to sorrow.
Burrowed deeply in our heart
Determine what is our part.
Melody, symphony, dirge.
What'll it be?
The onus is both on the sender and me.
Each free to choose the way of their path.
Forgive and let go?
Hold on and be bound?
What is your score?
What is your sound?
Consequences – count the cost!
Profit or loss?
A heart full of grief
Steals joy like a thief.
A heart full of love
Reaches out and fills spaces.
Replaces, embraces,
Chases the darkness.

UNITY

Reflected rays of sun
Casting shadows on my blinds
Warm the room with
Red tones of light.
Birds chirping, speak the language
Of creation.
"One for all and all for one,"
Buildings reaching skyward
Like the silent prayers of many hearts.
Awestruck by the majesty
Of one who knows all things,
Ever hopeful that their cries will be heard.
Now the shadows cloud
The light which still shines above.
Love penetrates the cover,
Wraps his arms around us
And hugs.

Epilogue: "...Perfect love drives out fear..." (1 John 4:18b – NIV)

NEW BIRTH

Seeds planted amidst the heart
Gain potential for a new start.
Spirit waters flood the gate.
Break down barriers of hate.
True religion begins.
Sparks ignite the rubble and
Burn the cords that strangle love,
Leave the stamp of God's likeness.
Stripes of healing
Evidence of Holy touches.
Fertile ash gives birth
To new leaves of hope
Bearing blooms of sweet aroma.
Gently fills our spaces
Returning us to Eden's graces.

A NEW SONG

Can you hear the faint melody
Of hearts reaching for the stars?
Gathering strength as the music rises.
Gently wafting on the breeze of contentment.
Soon to be loud praises of thanksgiving.
Filling our voices with harmonious notes
Of acclamation.
Eyes turned heavenward
As we seek our hope.
Expectation lifting us gently above the horizon.
Drawn together by trumpets' sound.
Homeward bound!

Epilogue: "And he will send his angels with a loud trumpet call, and they
will gather his elect from the four winds, from one end of the
heavens to the other." (Matthew 24:31 – NIV)

DOUBLE WAMMY

Swinging on a tree
Fruits of many colors sway.
Is this the price we pay
For dwelling on the fertile soil,
Working hard in daily toil?
Shades of black, brown, red and yellow
Just like the other fellow,
Live, breathe, hope and dream,
Drinking water from life's stream
That births all life not death and strife.
Won't you join hands with me?
Build together in unity?
See me as the one I am?
Not some horror doomed and damned.
I stretch my hands forth to you.
Together we can build anew.

JOY

Effervescent bubbles,
Light as a breeze,
Rising like yeast.
Spilling out of vessels,
Washing gently over all.
Lighten the burdens of many
Gives them hope again.

NEW BEGINNINGS

Upside down.
Roots showing.
No flowers here.
Nothing growing.
Life askew.
Old things swirling.
Vision blurred.
Tears flowing.
Cleansing waters flood
The landscape of a life.
Make the way
For future garden's beauty
To bloom in full array.

RAGE

Knows no limit.
Has no master.
Fires rampage.
Levels mountains.
Always seeking never finding.
Violent burning
Fuels the furnace further.
Desolation, destruction – brothers

Epilogue: This is no fire to warm yourself by.

THE BRIDEGROOM

Whispers of love
Leave trails of scented seed.
Sweet aroma draws us onward
Straining to catch the one
Whose mark lingers.
Gently, oh so gently
Woos us with beauty promised.
Encourages,
Reminds of dreams once firmly planted,
Now frayed by life's demands.
Sparks to life images
Held close within our heart.
Breath births fire in our soul.
Union makes us whole.

Epilogue: The spirit and the bride say, "Come!" And let him who hears
say "Come!" Whoever is thirsty, let him come; and whoever
wishes, let him take the free gift of the water of life.
(Rev. 22:17 – NIV)

A BETTER WAY

Trust no one, the saying goes,
Except yourself,
Doesn't matter if rhyme or prose.
Intent's the same—play the game
As if no one else knows a better way.
Who's to say?
The world's twisted.
Why weigh the consequences?
In the recesses of the mind,
Comes thought of a different kind.
Love your neighbor like yourself.
Don't put kindness on the shelf.
Think of others first.
Then I can pour out blessings
From the sky upon the earth
Once Eden's delight
Now a place for every fright.
Be bold!
A light in darkness shines.
A lighthouse among the tangled vines
Which strangle, entangle, mangle.
Caught in a vise
They cannot see
Fighting to be free.
The chorus chants to a steady beat.
Give Up! Let go!
You can stand the heat.
Truth's a lie! You can't win!
Follow us! It's no sin!
Ignore the stirring in your heart.
Don't do it! It's a false start.
Suddenly within,
I hear the strains of a violin.
Faint melody—other instruments joining in.
Sweet sound emerges.
Quells the urges so boldly stirred.
Harnesses the desire to err.
Floods my being,

A BETTER WAY (CONT'D.)

Clears my seeing,
Breaks my chains,
Voice now singing,
"Brother, sister, hold my hand.
Together we can conquer the land.
Justice, Mercy, Peace, will reign.
Joined in harmony, we can stand the strain."
Fabric weaving—adding strands.
Reaches out across the lands.
Spans the seas now with ease.
Voices raised triumphant
Drown the beat of chaos's thumping.

Epilogue: "I'm absolutely convinced that nothing – nothing living or dead
angelic or demonic today or tomorrow, high or low, thinkable or
unthinkable – absolutely nothing can get between us and God's love
because of the way that Jesus our Master has embraced us."
(Romans 8:38 - The Message)

Prologue: I awakened with the image of the sun and some lines from a worship song, "My God is an awesome God. He reigns in heaven above, in wisdom, power and might, my God is an awesome God."

MY GOD

Red ball of power and might
Visibly filling my sight.
Exciting my senses.
Fueling me to soar
Over fences founded in fear;
Trapped in tangled vines of feeling.
Encourages me to take
Giant steps forward.
Leaps of faith
Bounce me higher.
Skies no limit.
Eternity fills my horizon.
My God reigns!

A LOVE SONG

Like a cool summer breeze,
I love you.
Immersed in the sea of your love,
Sands of time stretch
Before me like the wind.
Never ceasing to be all it can.
Sets my hopes far beyond
The land's rise.
Fires my heartfelt desires
To the end.
Draws me close to your
Essence like a flame.
Leaves me strong in your
Presence once again.

Prologue: This poem is dedicated to my dear friend R.C. whose real life
experience inspired it.

A FATHER'S LOVE

Boy child cradled in arms so strong.
Clasped to his father's heart and bound by his love.
Heart touches heart and joins as one.
Father embraces this special son.
Love unbridled sparks flames of faith.
Cause him to conquer mountains untamed.
Stretches his reach to things unknown.
Prayers of anguish leap from his soul.
Cry out for his son to be whole.
Olympian speed catapults them
In a chariot of mercy sent from above.
Evidence of a father's great love.
Safely deposits at doors of grace
Where white robed angels enter their space.
Time spent here has pain of its own
Separating flesh from the bone.
Once together and now apart.
Torn asunder – heart from heart.
Son to his destiny ordained from the start.
Son now enters an arena of fear
Causing the heart to yearn for release.
Desire mounting looking for peace.
Piercing, probing, peering,
Twisting, turning, leering.
Disobedient flesh prevents escape
While the search for a cure causes others to gape.
Violation of sacredness occurs here.
Vision blurred as eyes begin to tear.
Wounding is deep and not easily seen
As the body struggles to reclaim its first gleam.
The scarring affects the issues of life.
Springing forth at odd times – causing internal strife.
Will spirit set free or soul hold with debris?
Though the heart wants to soar and searches for more

A FATHER'S LOVE (CONT'D.)

Fear still holds on – singing its song.
Spirit breaks through cleansing anew.
Healing takes place in this sacred space
Where God is the author and finisher of the race.

Epilogue: "But one thing I do: Forgetting what is behind and straining
toward what is ahead, I press on toward the goal to win the
prize for which God has called me heavenward
in Christ Jesus." (Philippians 4:13,14 –NIV)

FAITH, HOPE & TRUST

Hope and trust
Two sides of the coin.
Each by itself
Can't stand on its own.
Hope alone has no foundation.
Trust without hope has no direction.
Inextricably joined.
They leave room for faith
To balance them both
An act of divine grace.

DILEMMA

When spirit touches spirit
And souls unite as one
The story has just begun.

When a heart unfolds
Like an opening rose,
There is hope for the future.

When facts emerge
Contrary to the surge
Of forgotten expectations,
There is uncertainty.

How can this be?

As reality enters in
Uninvited as it is,
The propensity to err increases.
Desires clash with reason
Ascend to a season
Of struggle.

At other times, or so it seems,
Logic reigns as queen.
Will we survive these clashing drives?
Only time will tell.

This I know, full well
My heart is entrusted to my Creator above.
Master architect of love.
I rest in His embrace – fully!

Epilogue: "He will keep in perfect peace him whose mind is steadfast because he
    trusts in you." (Isaiah: 26:3 (NIV))

Prologue: "No branch can bear fruit by itself; it must remain in the vine.
Neither can you bear fruit unless you remain in me."
(John 15:4 b.c. - NIV)

LOVE IS

Love is the water of my garden,
The ripple of my brook,
The mist of my ocean,
And the rainbow of my sky.
It is the earth of my flower,
The mountain of my valley,
The dew of my grass,
And the leaves of my tree.
Without it,
I am a withered vine.

Epilogue: "He is like a tree planted by streams of water, which yields its
fruit in season and whose leaf does not wither. Whatever he
does prospers. (Psalm 1:3 - NIV)

AGAPE: UNCONDITIONAL LOVE

I choose to love you in
Clarity, adversity, and uncertainty.
I choose to love you when we
Understand each other and
When our eyes are clouded
With other visions.
To love and support you
Despite the circumstances
Is my choice.
You are deeply loved, highly respected
And esteemed.
Although perfection is not found
In any of us,
You are clearly traveling on this road.
You bless me in so many ways,
Conversation full of nuggets of
Insight and wisdom, encouragement,
And heartfelt laughter.
You bring joy into my life
And a feeling of completeness and competence.
Your sensitivity to my unspoken needs
Coupled with the ability to translate
This into appropriate action
Brings me continued wonderment and delight.
You challenge me to develop my talents
And fulfill my dreams.
Your presence in my life has expanded
My capacity to live fruitfully
And has given me hope for a greater future.
Best of all, you believe in me,
Respect me, and cherish me.
I drink of your fountain of love and I am refreshed.
In your presence, I can be myself
With all my contradictions and frailties.
You have proven yourself trustworthy.
When I am in your presence,
Pretense is not needed nor expected.
I am free to soar the universe.
Thank you for your love!

BROKEN

Like Humpty Dumpty, I was beyond repair.
One minute flying, the next naked and bare.
Stripped to the bone,
Flesh hanging like torn cloth,
Heart full of holes.
The winter wind blew through.
Death crept inside.
Once pride ruled as sovereign captain of this vessel
Now splintered on the rocks of life.
Waves crash against this once
Regal queen of the sea.
Warm memories cease to be.
Mind now frozen on barren landscape.

Up! Down! Up! Down! Up! Down!
No gentle rocking here.
Violent rhythms clash like cymbals –
Deafening sounds of existence.
Engulfed in pain resistance wanes.
Death calls gently like a lullaby.
Sleep away my child, sleep away.
Slip away my child slip away.
Rest here my child, rest here.
No cares my child, no cares.

Liar! Liar!
My soul cries out.
Shout stirring like wind-fanned flames of fire.
There's more to living.
I will not die.
Giving up's not an option.
Slowly, slowly, I rise within.
Held together by strings of others love.
Lifeline sent from above.
Gathering strength, I surface.
Waves now gentled.
I swim for the shore.

BROKEN (CONT'D.)

Epilogue: "He took some old rags and worn-out clothes from there and let them down with ropes to Jeremiah in the cistern. Ebed-Melech the Cushite said to Jeremiah, 'Put these old rags and worn-out clothes under your arms to pad the ropes,' and they pulled him up with the ropes and lifted him out of the cistern." (Jeremiah 38:11b-12...- NIV)

QUESTIONS

What shall I write about today?
Thoughts unbidden that continue to stray?
Long ago hidden deep in my heart.
Why arise now and encourage a false start?
Forgotten desires buried deep within
Surface today with powerful sting.
Answers elude like the breath of dawn
Linger a moment and flee like a fawn.
Faith! Oh Faith!
Where have you gone?
It's now that I need you
Don't leave me alone!

To dwell in the mind is very unkind.
Brings pain of its own from the seeds before sown.
Like the blind man, I long to see.
My God! My God! Help me!
To walk with courage the path you have chosen,
To leave my heart exposed not hardened and frozen,
To risk love again with its promise of gain,
To hope for a future where there may be much pain
And loss, unthinkable of course.
My destiny awaits me and encounter it I must.
In you, my God, I deposit my trust.
With you as my anchor, I will not capsize.
I press on for my high calling and my prize!

Epilogue: "… Forgetting what is behind and straining toward what is
ahead, I press on toward the goal to win the prize for
which God has called me heavenward in Christ Jesus."
(Philippians 4:13, 14 – NIV)

CONFLICT

Like a boat torn from its moorings in a stormy sea,
Violent emotions threaten to overturn me.
Suddenly ripped from its anchored hold
Into turbulent waters with dangers untold,
I fight to keep my soul!

Torn between two lovers a decision hovers.
Each one's embrace sweet to my heart.
Can I keep both and from neither depart?
That's the challenge or so it seems.
What about dreams? What about dreams?

Celestial light sent from above has captured my love.
Eternity promised in His embrace,
I long for His tender grace.
To disappoint Him brings grief and despair.
But His daily mercies offer repair.

My other lover brings comfort too.
Divine love embodied anew.
His touch so tender it melts my heart.
Remains with me when we're apart.
Like the bow in a master's hand
Strikes rich accord like no other can.
Melody! Harmony! Symphony!
Heavenly music are we.
Why discord in our duet?
Things from the past haunt us yet.
Conflicting desires arise in both.
True to ourselves or true to our oath?

Law versus Spirit – the eternal conflict.
Bondage or freedom – take your pick.
Each has a cost.
The price is high.
Pay it we must.
And, we must know why.
How will this end?

CONFLICT CON'T

Only God knows.
We must live in His presence
And grow,
Grow,
Grow!

PEACE

Search for her
Until she's found.
Priceless treasure,
Precious sound.
Always with us
All around.
Like air, she can't be seen.
Elusive touch,
Slippery sunbeam.
Essential, yes.
Easy, no.
Requires focus
To keep her so.

RESTORATION

That which was stolen
Was found today.
Unexpectedly given
In an unforeseen way.
Beautiful to my eyes
And, what a surprise!
All along God
Planned it for me.

How can I thank Him?
What words to express?
Allow me, my God
To not bring distress.
Not for any reason
Or in any season.
But let me bring love
Unfettered and free
To the one who has
Given it freely to me.

I love Him you know.
The seed that was planted
Continues to grow.
It's watered and fed
At just the right time.
In due season,
Good fruit he will find.

It's just the beginning.
There's much more to come.
Heart full of singing
All creation hums
Songs of the love
Of our Father and Son.

Epilogue: "In the fourth year all its fruit will be holy, an offering of praise
to the Lord. (Levitticus 19:24 - NIV)

IMPRISONED

Like waves crashing
Against the rocks,
Hearts beat frantically
Trying to be free.
Encased and bound.
Screaming agonized sound
Pierces the barrier of safety.
Flight to new horizons
Brings ecstasy.
Freedom's worth the price.

IDENTIFICATION

I feel your woundedness.
I send you blessedness.
Tender words dipped in blood,
Love, love, love.

Receive them in your heart.
Water of life, I impart.
Acts of sacrifice
Offered at great price.

Paid on Calvary.
Exposed for all to see.
Willingly,
I gave to save.

Agape's my other name.
Follow me and do the same.
Pour out your love for all,
That others too might hear the call.

My table's set.
The food displayed.
They sit and wait
Outside the gate.

Go out and bring
The captives in
To dine with me
The King of Kings.

CLOSED DOORS

Some doors open wide.
Warm rays of love invite you inside.
Others open part of the way.
Make you think you're welcome to stay.
Some remain closed indefinitely.
Requires your faith to believe that one day
With God's help they'll welcome you.
And when you arrive,
You'll enjoy the view
Is this a dream?
Or, does it only seem that way?
What else is there to say?
Except we choose to open our heart,
Those without are kept apart.
Unable to partake of the love
Of our Father above.
Expressed uniquely through each one
Chosen to represent His Son.
For each receives His call
To follow Him and welcome all.
Stranger, foe or friend,
We must extend our love to them
And follow our Shepherd to the end.

JOY! JOY! JOY!

What more can I ask for than
To be loved with a whole heart.
To be touched by fingers of love,
To experience closeness when apart.
To wake in the morning with thoughts
Of future joining,
To anticipate melodic chimes –
Notes played just for me.
To receive purposed arrows of blessing
Addressed to my attention.
To have uninterrupted connection,
To experience the beauty of focused direction.
To be cherished, respected, and cared for
In delightfully unexpected ways.
To be at the center of a universe
Created for two.
To have the sun shine even when
Its raining all around.
To have all these things
Gift wrapped in the perfect package
Is joy unspeakable.

Epilogue: "My cup runneth over. Surely goodness and mercy shall follow
me all the days of my life and I shall dwell in the house of the
Lord, forever". (Psalm 23 – KJV)

Prologue: Why are you downcast oh my soul? Hope in God.
(Psalm 42:11; 43:5)

ESCAPE

Moments of darkness
Creep in like shadows
Obscuring previously lit landscapes.
Sunlight's rays hidden from our view.
Warmth takes on a chilly character.
We curl up inside the womb of our self
Seeking to escape what might cause ice
To form around our core.
To expose ourselves is to risk immobility.
With great courage,
We reach out to our God.
His hand draws us gently to his bosom;
Warms us once again.

Epilogue: When the past threatens to obscure the present and obliterate the
future, we reach out to the God who is ever faithful to answer us and
deliver us from ourselves.

EXPECTATION

Here I am in my nakedness.
Fashioned by One who delights in makeovers.
Adept at taking broken pieces
As the essence of a new creation.
Atoms and molecules at His command
Precision dance to a new tune.
Form in ranks that challenge the Rockettes.
Every part synchronized and harmonized
With the melody of the tune maker
Who orchestrates an instrument of beauty
Waiting to be received by the one
Prepared to play a new song.
In eager expectation,
We wait for the wave of the conductor's baton.
The movement is about to begin.

LOVE FLOWERS

A flower blooms
Petal by petal
Until the fullness of
Its scent and beauty
Fills our senses.
Each step of its unfolding
Draws us towards its
Final unveiling.
In full display and clothed
In all its royal splendor,
We enjoy fulfilment.

Epilogue: "Beloved, now are we the sons of God, and it doth not yet appear what
we shall be: but we know that, when he shall appear, we shall be like
him; for we shall see Him as He is. (1 John: 3:2 – KJV)

THANKFULNESS

Tonight I slipped and fell
While rushing to keep an
Appointment with destiny.
The number 3 train
Masquerading one more time
Caused me to call on the Divine.
My body sprawled on concrete bare
Wondering just how I got there.
Embarrassed, I acted aloof.
Didn't want anyone to see me goof.
Wrist in new formation caused
New found elation to flee.
Anxiety began to overtake me.
Nausea creeping slowly into my throat,
Focus blurring,
Drenched in salt spray,
I wonder will I lose my way.
Do I let go and fade into nothingness
Or fight to hold onto myself?
With all my will I grasp the rock,
Cling to it lest I slip away.
Strength and vision return slowly.
I am encouraged.
I know God holds me in
The palm of His hand.
I am His.
I rest in His love.

Epilogue: I wrote this on the number 2 train after just breaking my wrist in a fall
on the wet platform at the 96th Street and Broadway station
underpass. I was in great pain and very faint.

WINGS OF LOVE

Holy Spirit whisper in my ear tonight.
Illuminate my vision bright.
Take me for a ride with you.
Lift me high in skies above,
Holy Spirit dove of love.
Show me Heaven's way,
Paths of mercy
So I will not stray.
Speak to me a vision clear.
Cleanse my heart so I can hear
Christ's sweet voice
Above the noise.
Guide me to the open door.
You alone know the plan
My father has for me.
I will never gain the prize
Except I press toward victory.

Epilogue: "I can do all things through Him who strengthens me."
(Philippians 4:13 – NAS)

Prologue: To those who are struggling.

VICTORY

He reaches out,
Embraces me
And takes me in his arms.
I want to run.
Instead, stand still.
My heart sounds no alarms.
God's peace surrounds
And shelters us.
The stormy sea subsides.
No longer torn,
My heart at ease.
I've finally won the prize.
Victory – how sweet the sound
To one who finally hears,
The voice of God who by Himself
Brings joy to those with tears.

Epilogue: "…in all these things, we are more than conquerors through Him who
loved us. (Romans 8:37 - NIV)

LONGING

Hidden desires long suppressed
Rise to the surface and disturb my rest
Persistent thoughts pop out of the blue.
When you least expect them,
They're right there with you.
Unlike feathers they don't float away.
But arise again on another day.
How to live in uncertainty?
Trust and more trust is the key.
It's the key to peace and serenity.
Each day we must start again
To trust God as we venture around the bend
Of life's crooked roads and dark hidden places.
And nooks and crannies of hidden spaces.
This is the wisdom I learn anew
To trust, trust, trust in you.

OVERFLOW

You fill me up with your love.
I expand to receive it.
I am full.

Drops of blessing tumble out.
Spilling over to others
In my path.

Fragrant molecules wash them.
The aroma fills the earth
With sweet scent.

Iridescent lightning bolts
Shimmer in the sky above.
Picture love.

GRACE

Creation awaits.
The love of God forever
Rests upon my soul.

FALL OUT

Like the fallout from a nuclear blast
Each of us is affected by our past.
Whether it be good or bad
Affects our perspective.
Makes us happy or sad.
Rain that's withheld stunts our growth.
Causes multitudes to take an ungodly oath.
Sunshine does the same.
Pushes many to live life as a game.
Where one-up-man-ship is the goal
Prevents our souls from being whole.
To hide our talents becomes the prize.
We refuse to participate in the exercise.
At all costs, we must stay hidden
Lest we expose ourselves to others bidding.
We've been burnt more than twice.
Now, we're reluctant to take others advice.
Soon the seeds of self-hatred are sown
And our very selves become unknown.
We stumble in darkness to find our course.
But, what we seek seems forever lost.
God in His mercy sends light our way.
Significant others who'll love and pray.
The prayers of the righteous avail much.
Love expressed outwardly is a healing touch.
They begin to build where others destroyed.
Love flows out and fills the void.
In time, a flood arises.
Opens the fountain of many surprises.
Gifts and talents begin to burst through.
Good things long forgotten begin anew.
Each discovery builds our trust.
Changes I won't to I must.
Now our course is truly set.
We believe we can and our dreams will be met.
Every life can be this way
When darkness flees and leaves the day.

FALL OUT (CONT'D.)

Be careful how you treat the weeds.
You're sowing life or death with your seeds.

Epilogue: "Death and life are in the power of the tongue, And those who love it
will eat its fruit." (Proverb 18:21 - NAS)

LOVE'S SCENT

Like bees in the meadow
Drawn by the sweetness of a flower,
Your scent draws me gently
Towards your presence.
Once there, I nestle in your warm embrace.
Your spirit envelopes mine.
Your essence permeates me and
Intermingles with my being.
We meet and fuse – become a new creation.
No longer separate,
One in purpose and form.
Points of light radiating God's love
Proclaim His majesty.

Epilogue: "The creation waits in eager expectation for the sons of God to be revealed." (Romans: 8:19 - NIV)

Prologue: Life is simple - life is difficult. The angle you view it from makes the difference.

PARADOXES

Kisses sweeter than honey
Worth more than gold or money.
As comfortable as your favorite slippers.
Hug your soul and caress your spirit.
Gentle winds blow warm breezes
On summer sands of love.
Clear blue skies that stretch forever,
Take us on a journey of vast universes.
Imagination stretched to the farthest reaches of our mind
Boggles logic and defeats our understanding.
Mathematics yields no magic formula.
One plus one used to be simple arithmetic.
Guess we forgot our algebra
Where X defines the outcome.

Epilogue: A promise from my God. "And if I go and prepare a place for you, I will come again and receive you to Myself; that where I am, there you may be also."(John 14:3 – NAS)

INTIMACY

Breakfast, lunch, dinner, tea
Sharing whatever happens to be.
No fear or concern
But open to learn one another.
Accepting, receiving, believing.
Just being and all that this means.
Touching, tasting, embracing.
Living water flows
And fills our emptiness.
Graces us with holy visitation.
Sparks the banked fire
Waiting to flame again.
Sun drenched earth
Warms the cold spots in our hearts.
Tender breezes whisper music
In our ears.
Helps us to shed the years
Of disappointment.
Fingers of love
Gently hold us close.
Create a shelter of refreshment.
We rest.
Later, the world calls us to our tasks.
Renewed, we embark and emerge again.

Epilogue: "That I may come unto you with joy by the will of God, and may with
you be refreshed". (Romans:15:32 - KJV)

BOUQUET

Bouquet of flowers.
Gift of love's earnest desires.
Bright blooms of beauty.

Red shouts, "Love Boldly!"
Pink speaks of gentle spirits.
White tells of pure hearts.

Purple tinged beauty.
A standout within the crowd.
Calls us to new life.

Prologue: A poem about my maternal grandmother.

BAMMY

My eyes fall on her picture.
This special woman of God.
Tears slip down my cheeks
Gently drip winding roads that etch my face.
Deep piercing stabs of longing
Interspersed with staccato bursts of
Tenderness and thanksgiving fill me.
Joy mixed with pain tumbles over my soul.
Bathes me in love.

Epilogue: "Greater love has no one than this, that one lay down his life for his friends." (John 15:13 - NIV)

Prologue: I was reminded of the plight of stroke victims. We, too, are
immobilized and need deliverance.

PURE LOVE

Speaks silently through movement.
Eyes convey messages
Plumbed from deep recesses
Beyond conscious control.
Truth screams to be heard.
Silence rings loudly in our soul
Proclaiming mysteries untold.
Pain unrecognized
Frustrates the universe.
Wreaks havoc with idealized vision
Fracture's the whole.
One chosen for the task
Sees beyond the mask.
Tenderly fashions
Instruments of renewed beauty.

Epilogue: "Your people will rebuild the ancient ruins and I will raise up the age-
old foundations; you will be called Repairer of Broken Walls,
Restorer of Streets with Dwellings."(Isaiah: 58:12 - KJV)

BE STILL

Be still!
Let the wisdom of God prevail.
Still your mind
And your soul's wail.
Let the light flow in.
This is how you win—
Success.

From the deep wells inside,
Life springs forth.
Pride is dispelled.
Turmoil quelled.
Whispers of peace
Make us well.

TRANSITION

Bridges to build and cross
Ease the pain of uncertainty.
Pioneer in a new land,
I fix my heart to journey onward.
Toolbox open and ready,
I wait for the blueprint's arrival.
Architectural plans set
In eternity
Shape my fragile frame.

LOVE'S CHOICES

To love when love is gain
And also when there's pain
Requires courage.
To rest in its embrace
When desire quickens the race
Demands trust.
To wait for future pleasure
While gazing at the treasure
Commands patience.
To seek one's desire
While courting other's ire
Involves risk.
To fulfill one's dream
When viewed as extreme
Develops fortitude.
Love's choices—
The building blocks of future edifices.

Epilogue: Follow God's spirit and you will find what you need.

TRUE SELF

Dewdrop in the ether
Glistening like a bright jewel
Perfectly shaped
Descends through earth's atmosphere.
Form altered by environment.
Reflective surface now crusted
And covered with soot.
Lands with a thud loud
Enough to rock the universe.
Summoned to quietness by
Many heralds,
Crescendo fades to decrescendo.
Faint echoes of origin pulsate.
Now and then break the
Ban of silence
Only to be quieted again.
Tumultuous years brew
A fermented pot of thwarted desires.
Inner being struggling to
Emerge from the darkness
Superimposed upon it.
Agitated atoms whirling
Against the external frame
Create untamed fire.
Internal pressure causes outbursts
Of un-channeled energy
Leaving permanent scars
Of battles won and lost.
Deliverance comes unexpectedly.
Lighted fire within
Penetrates the darkness.
Bursts forth to join eternity's
Jewel Maker.
Ancient glories now visible in a new creation
Blind the eyes with brilliant rainbows of beauty.

Epilogue: "Therefore, if anyone is in Christ, He is a new creation; the old has
gone the new has come". (II Corinthians: 5 -17 – NIV)

UNFULLFILLED DREAMS

I long to be refreshed by your spirit;
To hear the sound of your heartbeat against my ear.
To feel the smoothness of your skin against mine.
To melt into your presence—
At one with you and the universe.
To fall asleep in your arms
And awaken to find myself
Wrapped up in your beauty.
To feel your gentle touch
As your fingers trace paths on my soul.
To hear "I love you", whispered softly
As we nestle close together.
To hold your hand in public places
And not care what others think.
To caress your face and gaze deeply
Into your eyes.
I want to experience the fullness of our love
Over and over again.

MOVING ON

I hear the locomotive's sound
Beating out a rhythmic tune.
Whistle blowing for all to hear,
"Hop on board and see the country."
Like the Pied Piper's song,
My heartstrings are drawn to the melody.
Hypnotic chords pulsating.
Notes of new music drift before me.
Old songs haunt my memories
Growing fainter in the distance.
"All aboard", the conductor cries.
I climb the steps of my dreams.

Epilogue: "But whoever drinks the water I give him will never thirst. Indeed, the water I give him will become in him a spring of water welling up to eternal life". (John: 4:13 - NIV)

Prologue: I wrote this after returning from my first participation in an Open
Mike poetry reading.

BETRAYAL

Set up from the beginning,
Unsuspecting souls
Draw near to a hidden fire.
Outside appearances beckon
Sweetly with glittering baubles
Which dazzle the senses.
Children drawn to a Pied Piper
Of religious visions.
Having no experience with the real thing,
They fail to recognize a counterfeit.
Only when they feel their wings being scorched
Will they realize their plight.
Who will save the innocent?
You, Trumpet players,
Now's the time to blow your horns.

Epilogue: "Blow a trumpet in Zion, and sound the alarm on My holy mountain!
(Joel 2:1a – NAS)

DESIRES

Visions of freedom dance in my head
As I lie here supine on my bed.
What if? What if, I follow my mind?
Will life treat me well or be unkind?
These are the paths I long to explore.
But, somehow, I fear I might live to abhor.
The choices I've made some before.
Life, it ain't easy or didn't you know?
When it's lived out on earth here below.
There're choices to make and
They aren't always clear.
Also, the end can be sunny or drear.
The heart say's "Yes, fulfill your dreams."
The mind says, "Tread lightly or be carried downstream."
This is the paradox of life in this sphere
To separate ourselves or to draw near
To the eternal one
Who guides us each day.
Who leads us step-by-step on the way.
To the Cross, of course,
Where we face our real self
To decide to continue or be set on the shelf.
It's impossible to go back
When you've come this far.
But the pains of desire continue to spar
With the flame of the Eternal Star.

Epilogue: The struggle between fleshly desires and the spirit of God is real in our lives. "So I find this law at work: When I want to do good, evil is right there with me. For in my inner being, I delight in God's law, but I see another law at work in the members of my body, waging war against the law of my mind and making me a prisoner of the law of sin at work within my members." (Romans: 7:21-23 – NIV)

OASIS

Blue skies.
No rain.
Sunny hearts.
No pain.
Green grass.
Greener trees.
Fresh air.
Gives ease.
Turmoil gone.
Vision bright.
Revelation!
Clear sight.
God is here
In all we do.
Always loving
Me and you.

Epilogue: "Who shall separate us from the love of Christ?"
(Romans: 8:35a – NIV)

WHY I WORE THE PURPLE DRESS

I wanted to be a royal jewel adorning your arm,
To shine brilliantly and reflect your glory
And to make a bold statement which said,
"I am a woman."
I am a black and beautiful woman.
I am a sistuh who's lived to tell her story.
I am still writing chapters in my book of life.
The beginning of creation found me in the cosmos.
Waiting!
Waiting for my act to begin.
The trumpets blew.
The cymbals clashed.
I burst on stage to a flurry of drums
Into a kaleidoscope of color changing shapes.
Encounters of a different kind
Sought to obliterate my existence;
Hid my light and dimmed my soul.
I waited in darkness.
A torrent of life-giving water
Baptized me into myself.
Dislodged the moonless night sky
And moved me center stage.
HERE I AM!
Shining like the full cut diamond I was designed to be.
I am the warm earth
That nourishes the seed of life.
I am the milk and honey of the Promised Land.
In me, all things are held and birthed.
I am filled with the wisdom of the universe.
I am a depository of all that is good.
Seeds of love sown in my garden's fertile soil
Bring forth succulent golden fruit
Surpassed by none.
Taste and see that I am good.
In case you missed it, I wore the purple dress for you—
A sun-kissed god of the universe.
A jewel's setting enhances its brilliance.

Epilogue: "Oh, taste and see that the Lord is good; How blessed is the man who
takes refuge in Him! (Psalms: 34:8 – NAS)

CAMERA'S EYE

As I hold your hand
And soar through the universe,
I see worlds I never
Dreamed existed.
New horizons glimpsed
By eyes brightened
With spirit's sunshine
Beckon my now restless heart.
Music of my spirit leaps
To join new notes of
Creative redemption.
Familiar pieces blend with
Immortal songs known
Throughout eternity.
Haunting tunes quicken my senses
Like the smell of my favorite meal.
Cause me to taste my future.
Palate kissed by exquisite tastes
Insures my continued participation in the
Journey to the unknown.
Heart stirred in anticipation of gifts waiting to be opened
Energizes, revitalizes and directs my footsteps.
Eyes now focused on promised goals,
I move agily into my future.

Epilogue: "The sovereign Lord is my strength; he makes my feet like the feet of
a deer, he enables me to go on the heights" (Habakkuk: 3:19 – NIV)

WHEN I GROW UP

Prologue: Dedicated to "Miz Lucy" who is a colorful and challenging presence
in a gray world."

When I grow up, I'll be a princess.
Dress up in fine clothing,
Lot's of jewelry, wear fancy hairdos
And have all the shoes I want
When I grow up!
I'll have my knight in shining armor
Standing tall, spear in hand,
Ready to take on all suitors.
Lions will flee at the sight of him.
My door will be guarded from adversity.
When I grow up,
I'll feed the hungry, clothe the poor,
And build fine houses for people to live in.
When I grow up,
I'll sing lullabies to babies
Of all ages—zero to infinity,
Hold them in my arms
And rock, rock, oh so gently
So's not to wake them.
When I grow up,
I'll plant flowers,
Paint buildings in bold and bright colors
Reminiscent of tropical fauna,
And sell cloth fit for royalty.
When I grow up,
I'll sing and dance,
Twirl and swirl about,
Foot stomping, hand clapping
Rhythms of praise.
When I grow up,
I'll heal the sick, bring water to the thirsty,
Comfort the dying,
And strengthen the living
When I grow up.
When all the I's grow up,
Our world will be beautiful.

HEART BEAT

Yesterday, I felt your heart beat
As if it were my own.
Joined in rhythmic unity,
We played life's song.
Creative life flowed between us
Took us far away.
As we looked down on the earth,
We felt each other's birth.
Our love for one another
Has surely set us free
To follow God's own leading
Into our destiny.
In Him, there is no distance
But only cords of love
That bind us to each other
And to the one above.
Joined hand in hand
We scout the land
And settle where He leads.
We plant our gifts and water them.
And wait for them to flower.
But most of all, we feel
Your love no matter what the hour.
It comforts us and gives us joys
And sends us forth again,
To do the work we've been assigned
And to do it until the end.

Epilogue: Two are better than one, because they have a good return for
their labor: (Ecclesiastes: 4:9 – NAS)

THE MUSIC PLAYED ON

Joyous rhythm,
Blues beat,
Soul singing,
Intense heat.
Finger popping,
Shoulder shaking,
Foot tapping,
Spirit partaking.
Soaking sounds,
Senses stirred.
Exclamations!
Emotions whirred.
Creative juices
Flowing now.
Life's exciting
WOW!!!

Epilogue: I wrote this while attending a Summer Breeze Concert in
Mount Vernon, New York, while a thunderstorm raged outside.

DANCING ALONE

I love to dance.
It's in my blood.
Like oxygen,
I need it to survive.
I heard the band begin to play.
My body parts began to sway.
My heart beat fast.
My fingers tapped.
Before I knew it,
I was zapped
By the sounds of my spirit
Leaping to join the notes floating in the air.
I yearned to catch them like sunbeams.
To incorporate them into myself.
These were the sounds I recognized.
Reflections of the melodies and harmonies
That live within me.
I thought of times past
When partners of my spirit
Leaped to the same rhythms.
I thought of future movements and harmonious joining.
Point and counterpoint
Making music all our own.
In the meantime,
I DANCE ALONE.
The notes of my heart embrace those being played
By others of the same persuasion.
Like stars twinkling in a night sky
Or fireflies blinking in a darkened meadow,
We dance our tunes to our own score sheets.
While at the same time,
Others desire to learn our music.

I BELIEVE

I believe that dreams can become realities.
I believe that sunflowers grow.
I believe that roses can talk.
I believe they know God's walk.
I believe that rainbows are real.
And the pot of gold is God's own seal.
I believe that heartbeats write
Songs of love and dirges of strife.
I believe that a diamond's glitter
Often leads to a drought of bitter.
I believe in answers to be found
When we continue to listen to our heart's sound.
I believe that eternal hope
Is found in a special bar of soap
That washes us from all life's dirt.
And ushers us into a new birth.
It doesn't matter what package it's in
As long as we allow it to cleanse our sins.
In the eyes of man all things seem right.
But seen through God's eyes they become a fright
That forces us to shed the things of the past
And exchange them for gifts that will last.
Everyone journeys toward this end.
It always occurs when you round the bend.
Learn the lesson of life found here.
Love is always God's answer to fear.

Epilogue: "…Fear not, for the Lord thy God is with thee!"
(Genesis: 26:24 – KJV)

SUNBEAMS

I bask in the glow of your presence.
God of the universe who embraces me,
Holds me in His arms and sings,
Notes of love and melody.
Like a mother rocking her baby
Who coos and laughs contentedly,
God scoops me up into His lap
While I snuggle close to see
What new delights will come my way.
I rest in perfect security.
I melt into the rhythm of His heartbeat
And hear the voice of God's soul speak.
Whispers that surround me like mists of the night,
Banish my fears and break forth in great light.
I revel in the warmth of the sun,
Content and at peace,
Now that we're one.

Epilogue: "For in him we live, and move, and have our being…"
(Acts:17:28 - KJV)

REFUGE

Let me rest in the crook of your embrace
And leave no space between us.
Shrouded by earth's floating mists
And silky drops of velvet smoothness.
Spinning opaque webs of delight.
Warm me with your molten fire
That changes ice into life giving water,
Quenches my thirst as I inhale
Your scent of strength.
Perfect match to all my needs,
I find safety and rest in the
Cocoon of our love.

Epilogue: "O Lord, my strength, and my fortress, and my refuge in the day of affliction. (Jeremiah:16:19 - KJV)

WAITING

Waiting, we rest.
Waiting, we dream.
Waiting, we watch.
Waiting, we scream.
Waiting in pain.
Waiting brings gain.
Waiting, we see.
Waiting, we pray.
Waiting, we climb
Mountains of fear.
Waiting is good.
Waiting is hard.
Waiting brings growth.
Waiting! Waiting! Waiting!
Life's fertilizer for full bloomed flowers
Watered by our tears.

Epilogue: "They that wait upon the Lord shall renew their strength; they shall mount up with wings as eagles; they shall run, and not be weary; they shall walk and not faint . (Isaiah:40:31 - KJV)

WHO AM I?

I am a rose in full bloom
Not a witch on a broom.
A rare piece of music waiting
For the maestro's fingers
To evoke unheard melodies.
I span octaves.
From bass to high C describes me.
Variety!
You can't enclose me.
I escape your preconceptions
Like a child catching sunbeams.
When you open your hand,
I've traveled to another land.
Today, I'm a queen holding court.
Tomorrow—a soldier whose battle's well fought.
One minute gentle then roar like a lion.
Smiling sometimes and at other times crying.
Depending on who's playing my keys,
I relax and love with ease.
Dare to know me, I pray.
Stay, I say,
And partake of the richness
Of a full life's unfolding.

Epilogue: To open your heart and mind to God's expression through another is
to increase the treasures of your own life.

Prologue: During a spell of exhaustion, I went walking in the woods of the
             Bronx Botanical Gardens where the beauty of nature lifted my spirit.

BREAKTHROUGH

I saw the colors of autumn bright
Reflecting the brilliance of the light.
Lighting the sky and lifting my soul.
Giving clear guidance and making me bold.
Stirring the life that lives within.
Creating sweet songs that make me sing.
Writing the tunes that make me sane.
Harmony, melody dispelling the pain
Of living and giving until bone dry,
Of crying and whining and asking, Why?
Why me? Oh no! Let it pass by.
With moaning and groaning and then a sigh,
We finally stop and look above
And reach for the universe filled with love.
We inhale deeply the breath of our being.
The mist floats away and we end up now seeing.
How wonderful! How exuberant! How beautiful things are!
Renewing our faith, we reach for the star.

Epilogue: I worship you, O God, in the beauty of your creation.

BLESSED QUIETNESS

Quiet as whispers of morning mists
God's peace drapes like silken garments.
Caressing, embracing, invoking thanksgiving
Jeweled gifts offered by one worthy of honor.

Prologue: Pure love springs alive whenever hearts are open.

BANKED FIRES

I thought the flame had dwindled.
But how was I to know
That just below the surface
It continues on to grow.
Just when the ground looked bleak,
A bud began to peak
It's way through covered dark
Ignited by a spark
Of love's eternal flame
Embracing with no blame.
I marveled at the depth of care
That came from deep within.
Inhaled the scent of God's pure air
That cleanses us of sin.
It's love and only love that heals
And sets the captives free.
Fling wide the doors of your own heart
Begin again and see.

Epilogue: "There is therefore now no condemnation to them which are in Christ
Jesus, who walk not after the flesh, but after the spirit.
(Romans: 8:1 – KJV)

WINTER'S BLOOMS

Seeds planted long ago
Rest—awaiting their time to grow.
Hidden from sight
For future delight.
They'll blossom in Spring I know.
Others can't see what's dormant in me.
But I delight in God's vision and sight.
I'll be and be and be!

TRUST

As the blind man longs to see,
My fingers stretch to touch reality.
The memory of silken touch and gentle voice
Leave little choice.
Though time and space
May weigh the race,
I hope for your eternal embrace.
Unexpected waves of love change the pace.
I gently drift on seas so calm
And rest, relax, in healing balm.
Why can't it always be this way?
Why must we have these times apart
That stretch our faith and tear our heart?
Why times of dark instead of light
That cloud our soul and dim our sight?
It's needed child so you may grow.
Before we reap, we learn to sow.
All seeds must die; rest in the tomb.
First things first and then the bloom.
The earth's brown crust
Develops trust.

TIME

Time to smell the roses they say.
Time to decide our path and our way.
Time to absorb the Son's full light.
Time to say, like the blind man,
I've found my sight.
Time to put away tears shed before.
Time for the truth and not for lore.
Time to lead others to the One over all.
Time to bear fruit now,
Once and for all!
Time to stop playing and faking the walk.
Time to be real and live out the talk.
Time to shine brightly that others may live.
Time to give out now,
To Give, Give, and Give.

Epilogue: "To every thing there is a season, and a time to every purpose under
the heaven…" (Ecclesiastes: 3.1 – KJV)

BOWELS OF MERCY

Writhing in agony
My soul cries out to Thee.
My God, hear my silent tears.
Years of twisting, turning,
Yearning to be free.
Caged and bolted
Jailer has the key.
My God, my God,
Why have you forsaken me?
Eons ago I flung the world into space.
All things taken into account
Including that of grace.
I hear your cry!
I sent my Son.
Will you deny He is the one
Whose power leaves no lock undone?
Believe!
Receive!
The battle's won.

HEALING WATERS

River of life flows over me.
I drink of the tumultuous sea.
Debris spewing here and there.
Now and then, the water clear.
Thirsty, throat parched and dry.
Water! Water!
That's my cry.
Vultures circle.
I gasp for air—the power of life.
Sinking still amid the strife.
Clutching, clawing, too weak to cry.
Life's blood ebbing.
Slowly, slowly, letting go
Of life and woe.
Below the surface
Out of sight.
Drifting now into the night.
Darkness obscures all the light.
Destined for the abyss it seems
Cacophony of voices shriek.
Too late! Too late! Too weak!
Deep within a silent sound—torpedo forced
Bursts through the din.
Pretense, pride, nameless sin.
Jettisoned cargo strewn about.
Evidence of life's bouts.
Water's full—now all can see.
Driven to be all that life's created
ME!

CHAOS

Whirling, twirling, swirling.
Winning, spinning, sinning,
Coils of torment
Circling faster.
Twining, binding,
Tangling, strangling,
Wrapping, trapping.
Cords bind tighter.
Breathing's lighter.
Air grows scarcer.
Light now dimmer.
Darkness hovers.
Pulls the covers.

DECISIONS

Yes?
No?
Stop?
Go?
Maybe so.
Sighing.
Crying.
Hailing.
Wailing.
Stomach knotted,
Thoughts besotted.
Twisting, turning,
Ever learning.
Up!
Down!
Spinning round.
To and fro
Here we go.
Wit's end again.
Thoughts screeching,
Soul beseeching,
Spirit reaching,
Straining to be free.
Here am I, says He.
We long to pasture thee.
Rest within my fold.
I will make you whole,
Guide your steps.
Let love unfold.

Prologue: When life's pressures overwhelm us…

A HIDING PLACE

When sadness wells up inside of me,
Blurring my eyes so I can't see,
There's a place I long to be.
It's deep inside where I
Find refuge in Thee.
Trinity and me.
Entwined we.
Love embraces
All life's spaces.
Infinity's graces
Shield the places.
Where hurt abounds
Love surrounds.
Permeates heartaches.
Heals—seals.
Showers sprinkle
Every wrinkle ironed smooth.
Will surrendered.
Mercy extended.
Justice rendered.
Fabric mended.
Spirit soars
Silences roars
Of rough seas.
Calm ensues.
Peace imbues.
Me, Thee, We.

Epilogue: He who dwells in the shelter of the Most High shall abide under the
shadow of the Almighty. I will say of the Lord he is my refuge and
my fortress. My God in him will I trust. (Psalm 91:2 – NIV)

LIVING

Thrust into life's indignities;
Nothing gentle here.
Breath of life or fear
The death that's waiting near.
Straining for air,
Lungs about to burst.
Eternal thirst perpetuates
Then activates a life-long search.
Looking for I know not what.
Still driven to seek.
Now and then—nest and rest.
Life emerges.
Begins the quest again.

SAFETY

Walking along life's crooked paths.
Seeing what I can see.
Hearing the thunder claps loud in the sky.
Being who I can be.
Forgetting the sunrise that brightens my life.
The smell of the air distracting me.
Oblivious to dangers strewn around.
Land mines waiting to sound.
Lightening never strikes twice they say.
Lulled by false visions, I continue my way.
Danger lurks!
Disaster abounds!
Blinded by desire, I hear no alarm.
Others frantically seek my attention.
Trying to warn me of failed intention .
Vision clouded, I grope on my way.
Some continue to cry out and say,
"Slow down! Stop!
Before it's too late.
Wait! Wait! Wait!"

Epilogue: "But seek first his kingdom and his righteousness, and all these things
will be given unto you." (Matthew 6:33 - NIV)

Prologue: For those suffering alienation in their lives.

LONELINESS

Like raindrops splashing against a window,
Dirt and water mixed—streaking.
Stripes of seeing
Intermingled with darkness.
Brief encounters with souls seeking
Refreshment.
Momentary at oneness
Decreases then ceases.
Pangs of pain
Propel,
Provide.
Fuel us for future joinings.
We try again.

DREAMS

Start out unfocused.
Gradually take shape.
Propel us toward fulfillment.
Energize our wait.
Life events alter.
Change the picture seen.
Soon we forget
There ever was a dream.
When the struggle ceases
And there's time to rest,
The picture comes in focus
Sharp and at its best.
Now's the time to act.
Set our course again.
Continue to seek it.
And hope we reach the end.

MEDITATION AND PRAYER

I am, by nature, a part of God.
In God's presence,
I find respite and freedom.
Mind and soul rest.
In the stillness of God's spirit,
Creator and self join.
I am infused with life
As a fetus draws from its mother.
Peace enfolds me.
The quiet whisper of God's voice
Speaks as though it were my own.
I am content
In the womb of his presence.
Love fills me.
I trust the wisdom
Of the Power that guides me.
God is—I am.

METAMORPHOSIS

Our eyes
Meet
Across the room.

Our souls
Speak
Silent love sounds.

Our hearts
Leap
To greet each other.

Our lips
Touch
Molten streams.

A new
World
Creation sings.

LOVE CHILD

Passionate encounters
Joined in unity.
Hearts bonded in love,
Desires one,
Form love cords
Stretching to birth fruit.
In time,
Desire becomes flesh.
In awe,
We witness the Divine.

Epilogue: This is dedicated to my firstborn, Errol John Brown, Jr. May you always know the love of your father and mother who marveled at the beautiful creation of God's love—you.

Prologue: One morning a lone blackbird sitting in a tree caught my eye as I rode to work and the first two lines came to me. On another morning two months later, it was a water tower that caught my attention on the drive in to work and the first two lines of part two came into my mind. At the time, I didn't know the two parts would form one poem.

SENTINEL (Part I)

Lone blackbird sitting in a tree
Watching, wondering, who will it be?
Someone's destiny to set the world aflame.
Love sparks tenderness, joy and, acclaim.

SENTINEL (Part II)

Water tower standing tall.
Who's the fairest of them all?
Glittering drops of dew sparked gems
Reflecting sunlight when
They dare to pen.

Epilogue: I didn't have the faintest idea what this poem was really going to be about. Poets are observers, reflectors, and commentators on what they experience and as such are often surprised by the depth of revelation that surfaces when they put their pens to paper. This poem makes reference to a sentinel who is a soldier that guards the gate or entranceway to an area. In fact, poets use words, imagery, rhythm, impressions, and other means to call others to pay attention to certain things. In that sense, they are gatekeepers who keep information from being lost by reminding us to pay attention. This poem seems to remind me that I am inspired to write by the deep joy of my relationship with my creator. Perhaps, it will remind others that they too have something of worth to share with the world.

THE FIRE OF HIS LOVE

All consuming fire
Cascading over mountains
Like molten rock
Change the landscape of a heart.
Touched by love's eternal grace,
We bow before His glorious face.
Whispers of His love embrace
Our frozen places.
Melt the stones embedded deeply.
Releasing pains long forgotten.
Making room for joys unspeakable –
Consummate love.

Epilogue: May the fire of God's love melt every wounded heart and free us to
fully live our purpose; leaving indelible marks for others to follow.
Let us be lights on the path of life that others may find their way out
of darkness.

IN THE BEGINNING: DIVINE UNION

Love runs like molten lava through my veins.
Earth's banks cannot contain it.
Gathering momentum pushes mercilessly
Toward the final destination.
All consuming fire of love
Chases then embraces.
We are one!

Epilogue: Written in expectation of the fulfillment of our destiny.

UNKNOWN GARDENS

The twists and turns of life's roads
Yield strange surprises.
Balloons of opportunity
Drifting out of reach.
Tantalizing colors of heart's hopes
Seeking places of rest
From which to bloom again.
Fertile ground where seeds of faith
Are sown—then grown.
We wait for God's own crop to show.
Watered by our tears
And fed by our prayers,
Words of life seeping deep within
Form strong roots of strength bound together.
Prize flowers of God's love
Loom then bloom.

LOVE'S LURE

Gently, gently, I call you forward,
Stirring your slumber.
Awake, my love.
Awake to your heart's desire.
Fulfillment beckons you
To shed your outer garments –
Those things that encumber your spirit.
Grave clothes that keep you from your destiny.
Let them fall away at your feet.
Step out of them in the fullness of
Your unveiled beauty.

Epilogue: "Lazarus, come forth." (John 11:43 – NAS)

REALITY

I thought I couldn't love again.
You rocked my boat,
Shattered my perception,
And sky rocketed my emotions
To outer space and back again.
What a trip!
Before I could grab hold of my senses,
Collect my thoughts from the far ends of the earth,
And do a proper reality check,
You were back in my space again.

I felt like a helium balloon getting ready to pop.
While at the same time, I wanted to float away
On a current of excitement that continued to build.
One minute riding on air currents above the clouds.
The next struggling to surface above the waves.
Stability having long fled to another land.
My world was spinning out of control.
Questions arose as my emotions unfroze.
There was a thermal thaw taking place
Deep within my heart.

I could hear God say,
"Stay with the process.
I'm in control.
Follow where I lead you
To your own pot of gold.
I am the way.
Just pray and stay
On the path."

Encouraged, I took halting steps
Up a steep mountain path.
Each time I looked out over my shoulder,
The valley floor was a death drop below.
Caught between a rock and a hard place,
I pressed on to the mountaintop.
Climbing was arduous. A daily process of courage.
Along the way, there were many stones strewn.

REALITY (CONT'D.)

Some large – others mere pebbles.
The angels lifted me high above them
And set me gently down on the other side.
Free to walk and run again,
I leap for joy.

Epilogue: "Silver and gold have I none; but such as I have give I thee: In the name of Jesus Christ of Nazareth rise up and walk. (Acts 3:6 – KJV)

AGAINST ALL ODDS

Black man birthed in blood and pain
Seared by others' love of gain.
Mother's love guards soft spots.
Father's girds with steel.
Still, the pain is real.

Sealed deep inside
Real love abides.
Hidden from the self,
It dwells in covered places
Rarely felt.

Pride forces movement
Stirs us to achievement.
Accolades promenade like lovers.
Unfulfilled, the heart still stirs.

Forgotten dreams escape like feathers
Causing us to stretch to catch them.
Form building blocks to unseen places,
Release encrusted stones with many faces,
Opens us to unexpected graces.
Formerly occupied spaces leave room for love.

SUN DANCE

Yes, you danced for me.
The sky was your stage.
I looked toward the heavens
And saw your beauty bright.
Shining rays of brilliant orange
Ringed in flames of golden light.
You held my rapt attention.
My heart you did enfold.
You shimmered, bobbed, and weaved,
Bounced up and down again,
Hid behind the trees,
And surfaced now and then.
Your beauty was almost too much to bear.
But just when I would look away,
You'd dip again and sway.

Your music overwhelms me.
Your song's a pure delight.
Your voice is a soft sweet whisper
When I hear it day and night.
There is no other like you.
None can fill the space.
Except the one who made me
And fills it with His grace.

I've joined the dancer's circle
And choreographed my own.
Set to the symphony of my soul
Designed to make me whole.
I step into your warm embrace.
Your arms protect me now.
We circle worlds together.
My feet light as a feather.
We dip and bend, Leap and bow,
Twirl and swirl, Throughout the world.
We're one—you see
For eternity.

Epilogue: "Peace I leave with you; my peace I give you. I do not give to you as
the world gives. Do not let your hearts be troubled and do not be
afraid."   (John 14:27 – NIV)

CHILDREN

Children.
Creative,
Exuberant,
Compassionate,
Open,
Adventuresome,
Loyal,
Asking,
Exploring,
Absorbing,
Believing,
Expressing,
Caring,
Sharing,
Excelling,
Rebelling,
Dancing,
Prancing,
Singing,
Bringing
Forgiveness and
Energy for all life's living.

Epilogue: I thought about my preschool classes as I wrote this poem. I could see
my former students in my mind's eye as they went about their work of
just being themselves.

Prologue: This is a poem inspired by a French style of poetry called cinquain (sin-can) which simply means a five-line stanza. I used the format of one word for the first line, two words for the second line, three words for the third line, four words for the fourth line, and five words for the fifth line.

PAIN

Pain!
Goes deep.
Festering within me.
God makes me whole.
Removing sickness of my soul.

MORNING MUSE

Bright and beautiful are the stars of the morning.
Intensely brilliant, they glow.
'Til sun comes out—eclipses the show.
Or so it seems, you know.
Though the stars you no longer see,
They're now absorbed in sun's own energy.
When darkness comes—a part of life,
The stars shine out through the strife.
And once again, they light our path.
And give the gifts of love and laughter.

Epilogue: In all things, O Creator, we give thanks

Prologue: While walking through the celery farm in New Jersey, I saw a spectacular reflection and cosmic illusion on the lake. The sky was a magical and changing sky blue-pink purple that reflected in the mist on the water. It then began moving inland towards us. For a moment, it seemed that the mist was a hill and a lone duck was sitting on top of it as opposed to floating in the water. There was a sacred presence surrounding us in the hush of the moment. We could only look in awe and worship our Creator.

SKY BLUE PINK

Sky blue pink so magical but real.
Reach out and touch the raspberry mist
Of dreams come true.
Now you see it—then you don't.
Don't give up until you taste
The richness of fulfillment.

Epilogue: God's promises are yea and amen. (2 Corinthians 1:20 – NAS)

Prologue: These words began to form in my mind as I lay in bed (at Mount
Vernon Hospital) this morning reflecting on God's will for all his
children.

MIRROR IMAGE

I've just now seen the children
Whose eyes are blinded so
They see their very image
Wherever they may go.
Before they can be cured,
Their gaze must open wide
And look upon their siblings
Who're walking by their side.
They judge the world around them
By all that's in their heart.
And so they're doomed to failure
Before they even start.
The law of life is love.
It's always been that way.
It matters what you think
And also what you say.
Before a wrong is done
It starts with thoughts so small.
Then gradually you build a fence
That quickly turns into a wall.
You can't see what's behind it
Or even hear the sound
Of laughter, joy, and music
That's singing all around.
You wonder where the people went
And why you're left alone.
Search deep your heart within.
Uproot the heavy stones of sin
That keep the earth from bearing bloom,
Strangle growth, and leave no room.
Like gardeners weeding unwanted growth,
Remove debris and take an oath.
"To God alone I'll look for love,
Father, Son and Holy Dove."

Epilogue: My soul is free again to express through poetry. Praise God from
whom all blessings flow.

127

Prologue: "Two are better than one for they have a good return for their labor.
(Ecclesiastes 4:9 – NAS)

AFFIRMATION

A kiss, a touch, a hug divine
Brings life and love like molten wine
To souls that thirst and search
For touch and soothing earth.

Together we as one
Bask beneath the sun.
Rest our weary souls
While time's bell rings and tolls.
Restored we fly to different places
To share God's love and many graces.

Prologue: "…those who wait for the Lord will gain new strength; They will mount up with wings like eagles, they will run and not get tired, they will walk and not become weary". (Isaiah 40:31 – NAS)

SEARCH

Where are you my love?
Come into my presence.
Breathe on me.
Touch me with your
Life giving fire.
Quench my thirst.
Fill my spirit
And love me
Into fullness of life.

UNION

Fingers of love gently caress me.
Eyes of love drink of my cup.
Life giving waters spring up
Between us,
Refreshing our spirits—
United as one.
River of life flowing between us
Bursts past its banks and travels afar
Allowing the parched lands
To drink of its essence.
We water the earth that
Brings forth its fruit.

CROSSROADS OF COURAGE

We're not where we started
Nor where we hope to be.
We cannot see the future
Nor all that God can see.
We're faced with many choices
And need to pick the way
We'll journey on to fullness
From night time into day.
Which path shall we choose?
Which choice will we make?
Will we follow God's direction?
Or other's will we take?
To choose our own way
When anchored by grace,
Assures us of sailing at
Our own speed and pace.
The alternate road
Gives illusion of peace.
As soon as we take it
We're no longer at ease.
The path becomes darkened.
The road full of stones.
We grope in our blindness.
Fear permeates our bones.
We're tossed to and fro.
Our way is unclear.
We cry out in anguish,
"My God, can't you hear?
Help me somebody
I've strayed off the path
I'm caught in a twister
With grim aftermath."
Reach out for the safety net
Thrown within reach.
Grab hold of it tight
And swim for the beach.
Thank God I'm alive
And I made the right choice
To cry out, "Please save me,"

CROSSROADS OF COURAGE (CONT'D.)

In my loudest voice.
The choice that I've made
Leads to a new way.
One full of good fruit
And with excellent pay.
Eternal rewards as well as some now,
Lead to great joy.
Put your hands to the plow.

Prologue: I was inspired by the colorful bulletin of the Gospel Choir's uplifting concert held at my job.

COLORS

Red and white colors skyrocketing
Off the paper of life's dilemmas.
Startling contrasts pulling apart the seams
And forcing a hard look inside the fabric.
Will it hold under pressure
Or disintegrate like Bounty's Rival
Under faucet streams of
Living water?

Epilogue: To God be the Glory – Great things He has done!

SECOND CHANCES

Each day a new beginning.
Awakening dawn brings refreshment.
Hope bubbles like simmering pots of stew.
Mingled aromas of many kinds
Stimulate our appetite for living.
Nourish and sustain us,
Bring us into fruit laden places
Where we can eat again.

Epilogue: Your mercies, O God, are new every morning.

Prologue: "I will bless the Lord at all times. His praise shall continually be in my mouth." (Psalms 34:1 – KJV)

HELP IS ON THE WAY

When all is bleak and everything
Is dark around you.
When clouds are gray
And skies of blue are
Out of view.
And heart screams out
"What shall I do?"
There is God.

Prologue: I recently read two books dealing with families and their effect on their children. This sparked many thoughts about the family and the dances it creates—some positive and life giving and others that strain and hurt the body.

FAMILIES

Families made of woe and strife
Dance around the circle of life
Causing blindness so we can't see
Leaving holes in you and me.
Others dance with zeal and zest
Helping us to do our best.
Vision clear and ears alert
Healing us when we are hurt,
Loving us with all their might,
Teaching us by doing right.
Eternal flame sets all aglow.
Inner self soul seems to know.
Searches, seeks, and hopes to find
Others with love's peace of mind.
No matter what your origins are,
All can heal and travel far
By joining God-Creator's group
And doing our dance in sync with God's troupe.
Each one with steps individually done
Joins others and begins the fun
Of dancing, prancing, swirling and praying,
Leaping, twirling, singing, and saying.
Enter the circle of life my friend.
The one where dances never end.
There's joy and hope and peace galore.
There's love and health and so much more.
Come quick! Come now! Don't delay!
We need you to complete our day.
This dance of life that flows and flows
Keeps moving, changing—continually grows.
Creating life and sowing love,
We reflect our Maker's light above.

Epilogue: Written with thanksgiving from one who's learned to dance in freedom.

EMBERS

Can love's fire flame again
When wind's breezes futile seem
To scatter bits of heat
Where hearts once as one did beat?
Or will the cold winds blow
And strew the ash like snow
To heap upon the fire
Once fueled by heart's desire?
Can one plus one be one?
Will songs of joyful notes be sung?
Or funeral dirge bewail
And boat once moored take down its sail?

Epilogue: God's breath upon the ashes will ignite the flames of living.

137

CHILDHOOD

When I was just a little girl,
I dreamed I was a fairy
Who flew around the town by day
And didn't have to hurry.
While grandma stood at the sink,
I was wearing fairy pink.
Twinkling stars upon my head.
Sunshine beaming bright instead
Of darkness where the monsters dwell
And horrid visions burst from hell.
My heart was full of joy and peace
And lightness made my life at ease.
One day a rude awakening came
And things were never quite the same.
My world turned round and topsy-turvy.
My life's straight path became quite curvy.
Where things were clear and easy to see
They now were hidden and hard to be.
The clouds were dark, grey and stormy.
The sky not clear and winds not balmy.
Fear began to capture me.
I was bound—no longer free.
I lived my days in fear of night
When horrid pictures filled my sight.
No longer free to run and dream
My insides twisted around a scream.
It pushed its way down deep inside
Then soon began to build false pride.
Although I'm hurt, I'll never tell
I'll make them think that all is well.
So smile I did and make pretend
That all was right and would never end.
The years began to take their toil.
Where once things grew, there was a hardened soil.
My fate was sealed or so it seemed
Until God's hand intervened.
Pulled the stopper from my soul
Uncovering a gaping hole
Where stored up tears poured out a torrent

CHILDHOOD (CONT'D)

Of ugly feelings now abhorrent.
I never knew I felt this way
Until the bright light made it day.
My spirit soared and now was free
Just like the girl who used to see
So many good things all around
As she fluttered her wings to celestial sound.
Unencumbered, fetter free,
Light as a feather, she's free to be.

Epilogue: "Whom the Son sets free is free indeed. (John 8:36 – NIV)

LIFE NOTES

I rest in the bosom of the music of my life.
Chords of discontent rise and fall
Like sea swells licking the shore line.
Other times bring peaceful moments
Of lullaby's crooning.
I am gently rocked in rhythms so faint
I rest in fetal like fluid.
Encapsulated by shock absorbing love,
I surf the waves of life's events.

Epilogue: Life is like the sea. Beneath the calm is unseen movement that breaks through unpredictably and causes turbulence bringing with it hidden things that need attention. This brings cleansing and transformation. When the waves subside and the storm ceases, there is much peace and life becomes beautiful again.

Prologue: I woke up from napping while on the train to Greenlawn, New York to visit my parents. I saw this picture perfect circle of tall trees just budding.

WITNESS

A stand of trees
So stately and upright.
Witnesses of the truth
Still to be acknowledged by many.
Bearing testimony
To life's many mysteries.
Pointing the way
To universes unknown.
The sky's the limit is not all there is.
Why put a ceiling on infinity?

KEYHOLE TO REALITY

Bending down, I stoop to see
What images form reality.
Perception formed by boundaries ancient.
Cast in rough hewn stone.
Boulders large and small
Call out for change and stretching.
Yet, I only guess what fullness lies
On the other side.

Epilogue: A keyhole provides limited vision but this encourages us to open the door and see the fullness of opportunity awaiting us.

Prologue: The stopper that was holding the flood of words from coming out has
been removed.

LOVE

Love.
Our essence.
Flows through us.
Makes me feel safe.
I desire it's warm fire.

Epilogue: "They that wait upon the Lord shall renew their strength; they shall
mount up with wings as eagles; they shall run, and not be weary;
they shall walk and not faint." (Isaiah 40:31 – KJV)

A SONG OF LOVE

Holy Spirit,
Wooer of my soul.
Come and hold me
Make me whole.
Gather scattered pieces,
Fragments of my life.
Be the glue that holds me.
Give me peace instead of strife.
Caress and love me always.
Don't let me run—or escape.
Love me into the promise
Of God who gives me grace.
Restorer of all things.
Repairer of the breach.
Come and love me fully.
Don't let me out of your reach.
Keep me close to the Father's heart.
Strengthen me for a new start.
Guide my footsteps along the way.
Teach me how to hear and pray.
Help me answer God's call
To love others—one and all.

ADVENTURE

What new adventure shall I encounter today
As I entrust myself to God's own way?
I find it hard to wait.
I'm anxious to discover my fate.
Uneventful series of events I pray.
No crisis or problems as my pay.
In God, I trust.
I must! I must!
Where else can I place my faith?
Not in others or myself.
Just in my God, who else?
He is faithful and always hears.
Answers me before my tears.
Holds my hand and comforts me.
Gives me vision when I can't see.
Goes before me and shines his light
So I don't stumble in the night.
I'll enter into God's rest.
Depend on him and pass the test.
This is faith at its best.

BOUNDARIES

And act of God's grace.
Places value on our space.
Leads us to freedom.

Some are movable.
Depending on agreement.
Peace is established.

Others are rigid.
They are fixed in their stanchions.
Movement requires force.

Which form is better?
This we cannot know until
We test the waters.

Epilogue: "There is a way that seems right to a man but in the end it leads to death." (Proverbs: 14:12 - NIV)

PLAY IT BY EAR

Let the voice of God's spirit guide your feet.
The sweet whisper of God's peace be your meat.
Soft and gentle breeze caressing your soul
And soothing your senses.
Brings joy unspeakable in God's presence.
Arms of love cradle you close to
Heartbeats of eternal comfort.
And soothe the cadence of discordant music
Bringing melody where chaos reigned.
Restoring us over and over again.
Play it by ear today.
Let God's direction be your protection.
In a world full of many voices,
Let God's spirit guide your choices.

Epilogue: "…because those who are led by the Spirit of God are sons of God." (Romans 8:14 – NIV)

GOD'S BREATH

I sing of sorrows past
And those still to come.
But in the span between
A song of joy I hum.
It's always deep within
And helps my spirit soar
High above the tree tops
Through earth's chaotic roar.
The steady drumbeat of my soul
Stirs me deep within
To journey on to new dreams
Fulfilling them and then
To stop and pause,
Drink deeply of life's air.
Revitalized and refreshed
Restored in good repair.

Prologue: A song from the heart.

INVITATION

Spirit come flow over us
Like waves crashing on the sand.
Cleanse our sins,
Heal our land,
Refreshing us to once again
Proclaim your beauty
And your name.
Rejoice and bow
Before our king!

RESTORATION: MADE WHOLE

Born with a hole in my heart.
Parents tossed and torn apart.
No fault of mine;
Thrown into time
To live or die.
No understanding, "Why?"
But then, a hand reaches down
And scoops me up
Like a loving owner
Cradles their pup.
Holds me close to a heart
Beating warmth.
Breathes on me the
Hot breath of love.

HOPE

Lightening never strikes twice they say
But what about darkness overcoming the day?
Those are the times we're compelled to pray.
To seek our God and say,
"You are the light
And you are the way."

ON HOLD

Trading water—marking time
Waves bobbing—I grip the line.
Holding steady, I try to see
The distant object—my reality.
Sometimes clear.
At other times foggy.
Dunked in the surf
Wet and soggy.
A burst of energy fuels my flight.
Dry land now in sight.
In spite of obstacles, I made it in.
Now's my chance to score and win.

Epilogue: Sometimes the act of writing requires everything in you to push out words on paper. Perseverance and faith are needed to prevent giving up. Praise God for helping me express my struggle.

AWAKENING

Stir the sleeping giant that
Rests within.
Send a breath of fire
Cleanse the sin.
Expose the dirt and grime.
Do it quickly for the time
Is running out
And then the end!

Epilogue: "…greater is He that is in you, than he that is in the world."
(1 John 4:4 – KJV)

Prologue: I wrote this while vacationing with a friend at the beach in
Ocean Grove, New Jersey.

PETALS OF PRAISE

Petals of praise
And prudent promises.
Kindred spirits in the
Garden of Life.
Fragrant breezes refresh
The weary.
Sustaining our spirits
And lifting our wings.
Sweet aromas
Mingle together.
Leave a lingering scent
Of energy Divine
That rises to the heavens
As acceptable sacrifice.
Pleasing our God
And freeing our souls.

RESURRECTION

Pain so sharp it takes my breath away.
Gasping for air, I try to pray.
Words fired like bullets
Shriek through the air.
Hit the target
And tear.
Noise so deafening
I cover my ears
Lest my heart burst open
And pour forth the tears.
Dignity escapes me
As I reach out and try
To cover my woundedness
And smother my cry.
I must prevent this exposure
Or crumble and die.
What shall I do?
Where shall I go?
How shall I live?
Can I continue to grow?
Trapped in my pain.
Writhing in torment.
Longing for death
Not able to bear life
For one more moment.
No way of escape.
Face it, embrace it,
The seeds have been sown.
The deeds are now known.
What fruit shall they bear?
And how will I care
For the lives now affected?
So shattered and torn
Whose hearts' full of anguish,
Unable to mourn
For the hope once envisioned
Now covered with scorn.
Who will help them
Heal from the attack?

RESURRECTION (CONT'D.)

Bodies now scarred by shrapnel.
There's no turning back.
My maker, My God,
The one who knows all.
Can he hear me now?
Will he answer my heart's call?
Before I cry out,
He sends rain on the drought.
He sows love, peace and comfort,
Removes splinters of doubt.
Fills me with hope,
Lifts me out of despair,
Sends forth His anointing,
I now breathe fresh air.
The pain now subsided.
My eyes are now clear.
I see sun on the horizon
Have hope and not fear.
I'm learning to trust
In things large and small.
The fruit He produces
Outshines them all.
One day I will tell the world
How good He has been
When darkness covered my land
And the sunlight came in!

Epilogue: Written in grateful appreciation to the one who gave me the gift of poetry, my Lord and my Savior, Jesus Christ. To God be all the glory!

FIREFLIES

Fireflies drawn to light in darkness
Flit busily around its core.
Briefly light and fly away.
Can't stay long or so they say,
Or wings would burn and hinder them.
A little of God's flame is
Enough to ignite a torch
The whole world can see by.
When fuel runs low
And the lamp gets dim,
They draw nigh again and glow brightly.
Together they light the way
For those still prone to stray.

Prologue: When asked if I would give a reading about the life of Marian Anderson, I felt an urge to write this poem. It came as a surprise since I didn't think I had been affected by her life in such a personal way.

TIME STOOD STILL

She made her mark in time.
Vocal cords stretched to the heavens above.
Notes soaring like so many birds rushing south for the winter.
Fragrant offerings fit for a king and queen too.
Poised and still.
Waiting, waiting for the right moment
To begin her song.
A song of freedom hard won.
A score of sounds beaten into a melody shaped by life.
A song only she could sing.
Unforgettable—that unique sound only she could make.
Others make music too.
But this one soared into the universe.
Embraced by creation.
And time stood still.
If we listen real carefully,
We can still hear her music.

SOUL TALK

When my lips are silent
And my soul longs to speak,
I wait for you to articulate
The navigation of my journey.
You travel through this unknown terrain
As if you've journeyed there
Again and again.
You know the heartfelt feelings.
You feel the joy and pain.
You speak the language of my heart
And help me to be sane.
When darkness looms around my head,
You shine your light instead.
And, illuminate a passageway
Safe and sound—I can tread.
No matter what my issues are
You see and hear them clearly.
You point the way.
Go or stay.
Run or walk.
Let's talk.
I hope I do the same for you.
But this I know is true.
We speak the language of our love.
Spirits united by a Holy Dove.

Epilogue: God places special people in our lives who help us articulate the inner
journey of our heart. May each one find one who can help them make
sense of their voyage.

Prologue: "But love covers all transgressions." (Proverbs 10:12 – NAS)

This poem was written after my sister Diane and I met for the first time.

REUNION

Sisters long separated
Meet and greet one another.
Embrace face to face.
Destiny fulfilled.
Grace completes the circle.
Puts together what no man
Should separate.
Divine will prevails.
Once longing for connection
Now joined in perfection.
We walk hand in hand.
New horizon dawning.
Heart to heart and soul to soul
Our spirits one—now whole.

Epilogue: Blood is thicker than water. What God has joined together let no one separate. The sum of the parts is greater than each alone.

CANOPY OF LOVE

Sitting under a canopy of love,
Branches high and extended far above,
Surrounded by the warmth
Of the Spirit-Dove.
Strengthens me for life's
Continued race.
I draw deeply of the Divine breath
That powers my being and moves
Me again towards my death,
Not of body but of will.
I am drawn once again to be still
And behold the greatness
Of the God I serve.
I thank Him for His wonderful word,
Jesus Christ, My Savior and Lord.
In quietness and rest
My strength now returns.
I experience His presence
For which my heart always yearns.
Filled to overflowing,
I now can give out
To all I encounter
As I travel about.
In awe, I extol Him and
Lift His name high.
To God be the glory,
I press on for the prize.

Epilogue: "Be still, and know that I am God…" (Psalm 46:10 – KJV))

THE GIFT

I offer you the nectar of my essence.
Sweet drink of the spirit of my love.
Springs of life that water desert places.
Drink often of the fount that quenches thirst.
Rest in the garden of my presence.
Eat of the fruit of my tree.
Let me embrace you in the circle of my love.
Dance! Dance! Dance!
With me.
Be! Be! Be!
BE FREE!

Epilogue: Let my lover come into His garden and taste its choice fruits."
(Song of Solomon 4:16 – NIV)

CPSIA information can be obtained at www.ICGtesting.com

264303BV00002B/2/P